Super Simple

punch & Kick

Healthy & Fun Activities to Move Your Body

Nancy Tuminelly

Contributing Physical Education Consultant, Linn Ahrendt, Power Play Education, Inc.
Consulting Editor, Diane Craig, M.A./Reading Specialist

A Division of ABDO

ABDO
Publishing Company

visit us at www.abdopublishing.com

Published by ABDO Publishing Company, a division of the ABDO Group, P.O. Box 398166, Minneapolis, Minnesota 55439. Copyright © 2012 by Abdo Consulting Group, Inc. International copyrights reserved in all countries. No part of this book may be reproduced in any form without written permission from the publisher. Super SandCastle™ is a trademark and logo of ABDO Publishing Company.

Printed in the United States of America, North Mankato, Minnesota
052011
092011

♻ PRINTED ON RECYCLED PAPER

Editor: Liz Salzmann
Content Development: Nancy Tuminelly, Linn Ahrendt
Cover and Interior Design and Production: Colleen Dolphin, Mighty Media, Inc.
Photo Credits: Colleen Dolphin, Shutterstock

The following manufacturers/names appearing in this book are trademarks:
Styrofoam®, Baden®

Library of Congress Cataloging-in-Publication Data

Tuminelly, Nancy, 1952-
  Super simple punch & kick : healthy & fun activities to move your body / Nancy Tuminelly.
     p. cm. -- (Super simple exercise)
  ISBN 978-1-61714-962-7
  1. Physical fitness for children--Juvenile literature. I. Title.
  GV443.T858 2012
  613.7'042--dc22
                                                    2011000965

Super SandCastle™ books are created by a team of professional educators, reading specialists, and content developers around five essential components—phonemic awareness, phonics, vocabulary, text comprehension, and fluency—to assist young readers as they develop reading skills and strategies and increase their general knowledge. All books are written, reviewed, and leveled for guided reading, early reading intervention, and Accelerated Reader® programs for use in shared, guided, and independent reading and writing activities to support a balanced approach to literacy instruction.

Note to Adults

This book is all about encouraging children to be active and play! Avoid having children compete against each other. At this age, the idea is for them to have fun and learn basic skills. Some of the activities in the book require adult assistance and/or permission. Make sure children play in appropriate spaces free of objects that can cause accidents or injuries. Stay with children at the park, playground, or mall, or when going for a walk. Make sure children wear appropriate shoes and clothing for comfort and ease of movement.

Contents

3

Time to Punch & Kick!

Being active is one part of being healthy. You should move your body for at least one hour every day! You don't have to do it all at one time. It all adds up.

Being active gives you **energy** and helps your body grow strong. There are super simple ways to move your body. Two of them are **punching** and kicking. This book has fun and easy activities to get you started. Try them or make up your own.

Do You Know?
Being Active Helps You

1 be more relaxed and less stressed

2 feel better about yourself and what you can do

3 be more ready to learn and do well in school

4 rest better and sleep well at night

5 build strong bones, **muscles**, and joints

So turn off the TV, computer, or phone. Get up and start **punching** and **kicking**!

Muscle Mania

You have **muscles** all over your body. You use them whenever you move any part of your body. The more you move your muscles, the stronger they get!

shoulder

arm

neck

stomach

chest

back

upper leg

lower leg

Healthy Eating

You need **energy** to move your body. Good food gives your body energy. Some good foods are fruits, vegetables, milk, lean meat, fish, and bread. Foods such as pizza, hamburgers, French fries, and candy are okay sometimes. But you shouldn't eat them all the time.

Remember!

- ☑ Eating right every day is as important as being active every day

- ☑ Eat three healthy meals every day

- ☑ Eat five **servings** of fruits and vegetables every day

- ☑ Eat healthy snacks

- ☑ Eat fewer fast foods

- ☑ Drink a lot of water

- ☑ Eat less sugar, salt, and fat

Move It Chart

Make a chart to record how much time you spend doing things. Put your chart where you will see it often. This will help you remember to fill it out every day. See if you move your body at least an hour each day.

1 Put the title of your chart at the top of a piece of paper. Then put "Week of" and a line for the dates.

2 Make a chart with eight **columns**. Put "activity" at the top of the first column. Put the days of the week at the top of the other columns. Under "activity," list all of the things you do. Include sports, games, and **chores**. Don't forget the activities in this book! Put "total time" at the bottom. Make copies of the chart.

3 Start a new chart each week. Put the dates at the top.

4 Mark how much time you spend on each activity each day. Be creative! Use different colors, **symbols**, or clock faces. For example, a blue sticker could mean 15 minutes of movement. A purple sticker could mean 60 minutes of movement.

) = 10 minutes   ● = 30 minutes
    ● = 15 minutes   ● = 60 minutes

5 Add up each day's activity. Did you move your body at least an hour every day?

Tools & Supplies

Here are some of the things you will need to get started.

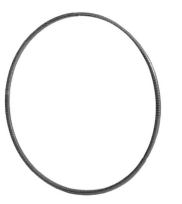

large plastic hoop

15 foot rope

markers

masking tape

craft sticks

foam ball

balloon

paper lunch bags

white sheet

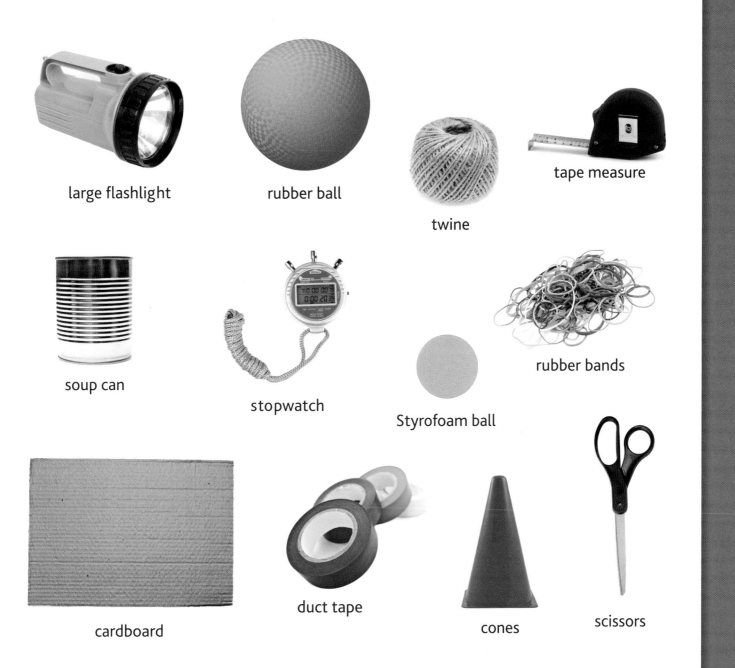

large flashlight

rubber ball

twine

tape measure

soup can

stopwatch

Styrofoam ball

rubber bands

cardboard

duct tape

cones

scissors

Balloon Tennis

Have fun playing like the pros!

WHAT YOU NEED

pencil
heavy cardboard
scissors
craft stick
masking tape
large balloon
string, 24 inches (61 cm)

MUSCLES USED

leg
arm
shoulder
back
stomach

TIME

10-15 minutes

Use a pencil to draw around your hand on the cardboard.

 Cut out the outline of your hand. Tape the craft stick to the cutout. This is your racket!

 Tie one end of the string to the craft stick.

 Blow up the balloon and tie the end. Tie the other end of the string to the balloon.

 Throw the balloon up in the air. Hit the balloon with the racket.

Try different swings. Overhead, backhand, underhand. Hit the balloon high and hit it low.

➡ The balloon might pop, so have some extras **handy**!

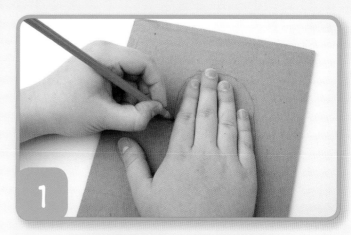

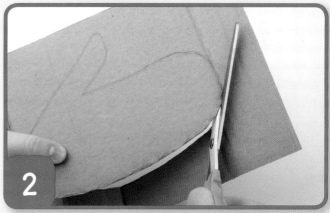

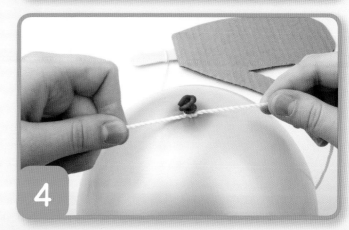

13

Balloon Kickboxing

A balloon makes a great punching and kicking bag!

WHAT YOU NEED

large balloon
string
masking tape

MUSCLES USED

leg
arm
shoulder
stomach
back

TIME

10-15 minutes

14

Blow up the balloon and tie the end. Tie the string to the balloon. Ask an adult to tape the string to the **ceiling**. Hang the balloon at eye level for **punching**. Lower the balloon to knee level for kicking.

 Punches. Make fists and hold them in front of your nose. Keep your elbows close to your body. Punch the balloon with one fist and then the other 10 times. Rest. Punch 10 more times.

 Front kicks. Step on your left leg. Kick the balloon quickly with your right foot. Bring it back to the floor. Kick five times with each foot.

 Side kicks. Turn so your left side faces the balloon. Lean away from the balloon, balancing on your right leg. Bend your left knee to your chest. Kick the balloon with your heel. Bend your knee back to your chest. Lower your foot to the floor. Kick five times. Then try your right foot.

15

Punches & Kicks

Fun and easy ways to learn how to punch and kick!

WHAT YOU NEED

just you

MUSCLES USED

leg
arm
shoulder
back
stomach

TIME

10-15 minutes

1 Air punches. Stand with your legs and knees together. Hold your fists in front of your chest. Bend your knees. Jump as high as you can. **Punch** both fists straight above your head. Do this 10 times.

 2 Bicycle kicks. Lie on the floor. Bend your knees and lift your legs in the air. Keep your arms at your sides. Quickly kick with your left leg and then your right leg. Pretend you are **pedaling** a bicycle. Kick 10 times with each leg.

 3 Rocking horse kicks. Stand on your left leg. Kick your right foot forward. Stand on your right leg. Kick your left foot backward. Do this 10 times. Then stand on your right leg. Kick your left foot forward. Stand on your left leg. Kick your right foot backward. Do this 10 times. Kick high and fast. Pretend you are kicking a rubber wall so your foot **bounces** back quickly.

17

Rubberball Soccer

A great neighborhood game that everyone can play!

WHAT YOU NEED

2-inch (5 cm)
  Styrofoam ball
rubber bands
4 cones
tape measure
watch or timer

MUSCLES USED

leg
arm

TIME

30 minutes

1 Wrap the rubber bands around the ball. Add rubber bands until the ball is 3 inches (8 cm) across.

2 Set up a field. Use cones to make a goal at each end. Put two cones 4 feet (1.2 m) apart for each goal.

3 **Divide** the players into two teams to play soccer. Run up and down the field. Kick the ball to your **teammates**.

4 Try to steal the ball from the other team. If there are enough players, have a goalie for each team.

5 Try to kick the ball through the goal. When one team makes a goal, the other team starts in the middle of the field with the ball. Play for 15 minutes. See who scores the most goals!

Kung Fu Shadows

Put on a show that will keep you moving!

WHAT YOU NEED

white sheet
large flashlight
rope
tape

MUSCLES USED

leg
arm
shoulder

TIME

10-15 minutes

Ask an adult to hang the sheet in the middle of the room. Make sure you can move around without bumping into things.

 Stand on one side of the sheet. Put the flashlight behind you. Shine the light so your shadow shows on the sheet. Turn off the other lights in the room.

 Jump kicks. Turn and jump. Land on your feet. Lean and kick sideways. **Switch** legs. Do each move five times and then 10 times. Keep moving until you are tired!

 Punches. Punch in different patterns. Start with left, left, right. Then punch right, right, left.

 Uppercut punches. Turn and punch up in the air. Switch arms.

Kick the Can

A favorite game everyone loves to play!

WHAT YOU NEED

backyard, park,
  or playground
3 or more players
coffee can, soup can,
  or plastic bottle
large plastic hula hoop

MUSCLES USED

leg

TIME

30 minutes

Put the hoop in the middle of the playing area. Put the can in the middle of the hoop.

 Decide who will be IT. IT stands by the hoop and closes his or her eyes. IT counts to 50 while everyone else hides.

 Then IT runs around looking for the others. When IT sees someone, he or she calls the person's name. Both run toward the can. They each try to be the first one to kick the can.

4. If IT kicks the can first, the other person is caught. He or she has to sit out. If the other person kicks the can, he or she can hide again. So can any players who were out. IT has to put the can back in the hoop.

5. There are two ways for the game to end. The first way is when everyone except IT is caught. The second way is when one person is caught three times.

Kick Golf

Who says you need clubs to play mini golf?

WHAT YOU NEED

paper
scissors
markers
6 paper lunch bags
6 craft sticks
tape
tape measure
Styrofoam ball
  for each player

MUSCLES USED

leg

TIME

20–30 minutes

Cut six triangle shapes out of paper for flags. Number the flags 1 to 6. Tape the flags to craft sticks.

2 Cut the top half off of each bag. Open the bags. Tape a flag to the bottom of each bag. The flag should stick up when the bag is on its side.

 Set up a mini golf course. Lay each bag on its side. Spread them out around the space. Put a piece of tape at least 6 feet (2 m) away from each hole.

 Each player gets a ball. Take turns kicking the balls to each hole. Begin with the ball on the tape for the first hole. Kick the ball toward the hole. Keep kicking it until it goes in the bag. Take the ball out. Go to the start of the next hole!

5 Count how many kicks it takes to get the ball in each hole. Play again. See if you can do it in fewer kicks.

Kickball

A fun game that's kind of like baseball and soccer combined!

WHAT YOU NEED

open space outdoors
8 or more players
rubber ball
duct tape
tape measure

MUSCLES USED

leg
arm
shoulder

TIME

20-30 minutes

The Field

1. Use duct tape to make the bases. Start with home plate. Then add first, second, and third bases. The bases should be about 60 feet (18 m) apart.

2. Mark the center with tape. This is the pitcher's mound.

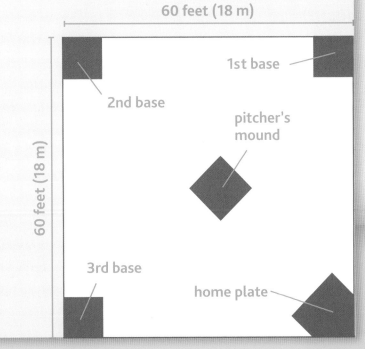

60 feet (18 m)

60 feet (18 m)

2nd base

1st base

pitcher's mound

3rd base

home plate

The Game!

1 **Divide** the group into two teams. One team starts in the field. The other team is at bat.

2 The first batter stands by home plate. The pitcher rolls the ball toward the plate. The batter kicks the ball. If the batter misses, it is a strike. If the batter gets three strikes, he or she is out. If the batter kicks the ball, he or she runs to first base.

3 When the batter kicks the ball, the fielders try to catch it. If the ball is caught before it touches the ground, the batter is out.

4 If one of the fielders picks up the ball, he or she can throw the ball at the runner. The runner is out if he or she gets hit before reaching the base. A fielder can also tag the runner with the ball.

5 The batting team keeps batting until there are three outs. Then it's the other team's turn to bat.

6 Keep playing until each team has batted five times.

A fielder may not throw the ball at a runner's head. A runner who gets hit in the head is not out.

Just Keep Moving!

Try these during TV and homework breaks, after meals, or anytime.

Karate Kicks

Make sure you have enough room. Kick your right leg to the right side. Keep your foot flat. Kick your right leg in front as high as you can. Kick your right leg to the back. **Switch** feet. Kick to the side, front, and back 10 times with each foot.

Punching Bag

Stand with your feet apart. **Punch** with your left fist. Then punch with your right fist. Pretend you are punching a bag. Punch straight out, level with your shoulders. Punch over your head. Punch down toward the floor.

Hacky Sack

Play by yourself or with others. Make sure nothing is in the way. Use your feet and knees to kick the hacky sack. The goal is to keep it from hitting the ground.

Being active is for everyone!
- Ask your family to join in activities at home.
- Have relay races with your classmates at recess.
- Have an adult take you to a safe park to play tag with friends.

Super Simple Moves
Pledge

I promise to be active and move my body for one hour a day, five days a week.
I know that eating right and getting enough sleep are also important.
I want to be healthy and have a strong body.

I will:

☑ keep track of my activities on a Move It Chart or something like it

☑ ask my friends to stay active with me and set up play times outside
three days a week

☑ ask my family to plan a physical activity one day a week

☑ limit my time watching TV and using the computer, except for homework

☑ get up and move my body during TV commercials and homework breaks

To print a pledge certificate, go to www.abdopublishing.com.
For more information about being active, please visit www.letsmove.gov.

31

Glossary

bounce – to spring up or back after hitting something.

ceiling – the upper surface or lining of a room.

chore – a regular job or task, such as cleaning your room.

column – one of the vertical rows in a table or chart.

divide – to separate into equal groups or parts.

energy – the ability to move, work, or play hard without getting tired.

handy – close by or easy to get.

muscle – the tissue connected to the bones that allows body parts to move.

pedal – to make a bike go by pushing the pedals with your feet.

punch – to hit with a closed fist.

serving – a single portion of food.

switch – to change from one thing to another.

symbol – an object or picture that stands for or represents something.

teammate – someone who is on your team.